The Tornado Story

▲
*RAF GR4 'bombs away'.
(Rob Howarth)*

➤
*Panavia Tornado up close
and personal. (Chris Ayre)*

➤➤
*Luftwaffe IDS Tornado,
43+18. (USAF)*

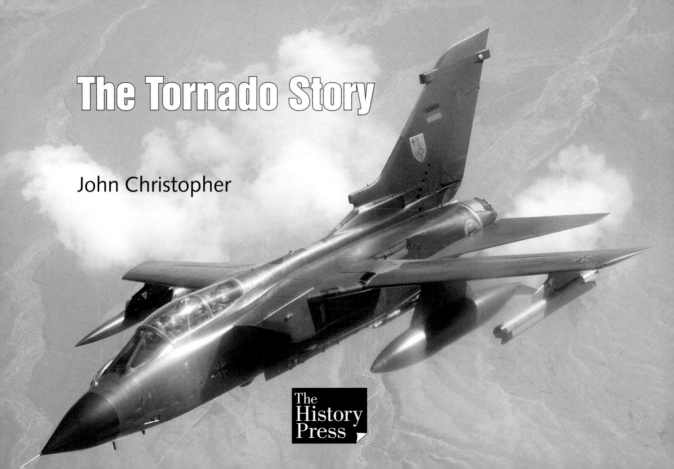

The Tornado Story

John Christopher

The
History
Press ▶

Royal Air Force GR4A refuelling during operations over Iraq in 2004. (USAF)

First published in the United Kingdom in 2009 by
The History Press
The Mill · Brimscombe Port ·
Stroud · Gloucestershire · GL5 2QG

Reprinted 2011

British Library Cataloguing in Publication Data
A catalogue record for this book is available from the British Library.

ISBN 978-0-7524-5085-8

Typesetting and origination by
The History Press
Printed in China

CONTENTS

ACKNOWLEDGEMENTS

Just as the Panavia Tornado is a wonderful example of a truly successful international collaboration, I am very grateful to the many international sources who have contributed the invaluable information and imagery which has come together in *The Tornado Story*. For photographs I must of course acknowledge Panavia Aircraft, British Aerospace (BAe), plus Motoren-und-Turbine Union (MTU) and Messerschmitt-Balkow-Blohm (MBB) of Germany, Lamborghini in Italy and the US Air Force, US Navy and the US Department of Defenses, for their enlightened attitude to the freedom of information.

In addition, I am indebted to a number of dedicated and talented aviation photographers who have generously allowed me to publish their pictures. These include: Andrea Agostini, Chris Ayre, Frank Grealish of IrishAirPics.com, Rob Howarth, Martin Hronsky, Melvin Jansen, Michal Kaczmarek, Mark McEwan, Stephen Messe, Adrian Pingstone and James Vaitkevicius. Many of the photographs in this book, especially of the prototypes and early production aircraft, have come from the archives of A.W. Kruger. I must also thank my wife Ute Christopher for proofreading and assistance with additional research, plus Anna and Jay for their continuing flow of good ideas.

John Christopher

Today the Tornado is recognised as a phenomenal flying machine, a multi-role combat aircraft that packs a punch way above its weight. Born of a tri-national collaboration between the UK, Germany and Italy, it has defied the skeptics by proving itself as a 'Jack of all trades' and master of them all. However, when it was first conceived, the notion of a truly multi-role aircraft represented a dramatic shift in mind-set away from all that had gone before.

Traditionally combat aircraft had evolved through two distinct and separate branches, the fighter and the bomber, and the perceived wisdom among many aviation experts was that to produce a single aircraft capable of carrying out both roles would result in one that excelled in neither. In the event the doubters couldn't have been more wrong: the Tornado has become the stuff of legend.

It all began in the late 1960s, a time when the Cold War was casting a long shadow of uncertainty and insecurity across the northern hemisphere and, in response, the air forces of several NATO countries were looking to replace their outmoded jets. For example, the UK had its squadrons of English Electric Lightning fighter aircraft, all-engine brutes that could take-off and climb at an almost vertical angle to intercept an incoming threat. And as a deterrent there was the fleet of assorted 'V' bombers, the Avro Vulcan, Handley Page's Victor and the Vickers Valiant – fine aircraft in their own right, but all ready to hand over to a new generation capable of taking on the challenges of the coming decades. For the RAF matters

➤

RAF GR4, ZD850, at Fairford in 2008. (Frank Grealish)

were exasperated in 1965 when the TSR.2 Tactical Strike and Reconnaissance project, once heralded as the successor to the Canberra, was unceremoniously scrapped by the government because of rising costs and delays. As the famous aeronautical engineer Sir Sidney Camm put it, 'All modern aircraft have four dimensions: span, length, height and politics.'

So it was left to the designers to create a new multi-role aircraft combining the maneuverability of an interceptor with the efficient cruise performance of a bomber. They did this by using a variable-geometry, or 'swing-wing', configuration. Sir Barnes Wallis had already pioneered the concept in the post-war years, and the French and British had worked together on a Anglo French Variable Geometry (AFVG) aircraft until France's withdrawal

in 1967. The following year Germany, the Netherlands, Belgium, Italy and Canada instigated studies on a replacement for the F-104 Starfighter to be known as the Multi Role Aircraft (MRA), later called the Multi Role Combat Aircraft (MRCA). Following some international shuffling Britain joined the project while Canada and Belgium pulled out. That left Britain, Germany, Italy and the Netherlands with the intention of jointly producing a single-seat *and* a two-seat strike fighter. Accordingly they formed Panavia Aircraft on 26 March 1969, although the Netherlands exited the scene the following year. A separate multinational company, known as Turbo Union, was formed in June 1970 to develop and build the RB199 turbofan engines.

By the conclusion of the project definition phase in the spring of 1970 two rival

concepts had emerged, known as the Panavia 100, a short-lived single-seater which Germany preferred, and the twin-seat Panavia 200, favoured by the RAF, which was briefly known as the Panther before it became the Tornado. In September 1971 the three remaining governments signed an Intention to Proceed, with development and production work to be split between Panavia's consortium partners with the British Aircraft Corporation (now British Aerospace) producing the front fuselage

'The Tornado has been developed to break the ever increasing cost-technology spiral. It has been designed from the outset to cover the entire spectrum of operations of a modern air force.'

Panavia Aircraft

and undertaking tail assembly in the UK, Messerschmitt-Bolkow-Blohm (MBB) in Germany making the centre fuselage, and Fiat (later Aeritalia, and now Alenia) in Italy responsible for the wings.

The result of this collaborative effort was a political and technical triumph, with the prototype, P.01, taking to the skies on 14 August 1974, and the first operational aircraft being delivered to the RAF and Luftwaffe in June 1979. In total 992 Tornados, including variants, have been built, and many of these will continue in service into the 2020s. This is their remarkable story.

◄
Two RAF Tornados flying in formation with a KC-135 Stratotanker over Iraq. (USAF)

An Italian IDS with the yellow lightning flash and diving eagle emblem of 36 Stormo. (USAF)

Faced with increasing task demand and spiraling development costs, it was clear from the outset that producing a multi-role aircraft for the 1980s, and several decades beyond, was going to be a tall order. For a start the list of specific roles was extensive; Battlefield Interdiction and Close Air Support, Interdiction/Strike and Naval Strike, Air Superiority, Reconnaissance, Training and Air Defence/Interdiction. Many critics at the time of the Multi Role Combat Aircraft's (MRCA) inception thought that the complexity and the politics of a multi-national design and production effort would result in a proverbial 'camel'. Once it had entered service, however, the Tornado emphatically silenced its detractors, and it continues to serve as a vital element in the air defence of the UK and the other operating countries of Germany, Italy and Saudi Arabia.

Artist's impression of the MRCA combat aircraft, pre-production. (Panavia)

Did you know?
In 1969 the MRCA was given the name 'Panther' before it became known as the Tornado.

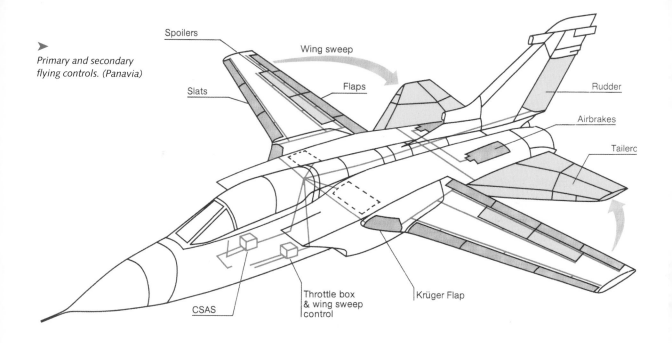

Primary and secondary flying controls. (Panavia)

Spoilers

Wing sweep

Slats

Flaps

Rudder

Airbrakes

Tailerc

CSAS

Throttle box
& wing sweep
control

Krüger Flap

○ Primary control surfaces
○ Secondary control surfaces
━━ Control runs
╌╌╌ Bleed air outlets

View of front cockpit interior taken on the assembly line at Manching, Germany. (MBB)

Tornado cockpit showing the TV tabs for the Weapons Systems Officer. (MBB)

3

The design of the Tornado was shaped by several fundamental elements, the most obvious being the two-man crew of pilot and a Weapons Systems Officer (WSO) in tandem, its compact size – thanks largely to the twin RB199 turbofans (see *Powerplant* section) – and its variable geometry swing-wing. Combine these factors with state-of-the-art radar and computing systems for flight control, navigation and weapons systems, and the result is a compact and versatile aircraft that can operate from small airfields and yet still carries a hefty range of weaponry making each and every strike count whatever the weather conditions, day or night.

With the wings fully swept forward lift is significantly increased for Short Take-Off and Landing (STOL) performance to enable the aircraft to operate from short runway spaces, which is considered essential as longer runways are more vulnerable to attack. For long endurance and loiter characteristics a moderately swept wing is preferable, while the fully swept back 'delta' wing is best for high-speed low-level flight with low gust response to provide a stable weapons platform and improved crew comfort. The latter is important in ensuring full crew efficiency when faced with a multitude of complex tasks.

On the IDS, the 'standard' model if you like, there are three levels of wing sweep – twenty-five, forty-five and sixty-seven

degrees of sweep – selected by the pilot through a lever in the cockpit, with the wings recessing into the fuselage through a simple elasticated rubber seal. The wing carry-through box is made of titanium for strength and fatigue resistance, and the loads are transferred to the moving wing by special bearings and pick up tracks. The remainder of the airframe is constructed mainly of conventional alloys using heavy frames and longerons to transfer the load through the structure.

Primary flight control of the Tornado is by means of two all-moving tailerons at the rear for pitch and roll control, with

Did you know?
Although unsuited to carrier operations the Tornado was fitted with an arrester hook at the rear of the fuselage.

▲
Prototype P.07 in preparation for a demonstration flight in 1978. (MBB)

'We started off with quite a number of nations on the project. In addition to the Italians, the Germans and ourselves, the Canadians were involved, the Dutch were involved and I think the Belgians.'

Sir Frederick Page, aircraft designer and chairman of Panavia

lateral control via a conventional tail rudder. Moving in unison, the tailerons can be tilted up or down to alter the pitch or angle of the aircraft, or, if moved differentially, they can induce a roll. At small wing sweep angles the tailerons are augmented by extensive flaps on the wings to give additional roll control. Secondary control surfaces, including leading edge flaps and large air-brakes on either side of the upper fuselage, are operated during landing to increase lift and to slow the aircraft down. The Tornado is not fitted with a parachute brake, but does have an arrestor hook, although it was never intended for carrier use.

The Tornado was the first combat aircraft equipped with a fly-by-wire control system, a significant innovation at the time. Inputs from the pilot's controls feed electrical signals to the Command Stability Augmentation System (CSAS) which receives feedback signals from the control actuators indicating their current status, with pitch, roll and yaw rates being sensed by triple gyros. The CSAS also ensures that the pilot is receiving appropriate feedback on his controls throughout the flight envelope. In the case of a catastrophic systems failure, possibly caused by combat damage, a fully duplicated back-up hydraulic control system provides a basic 'get-you-home' service. And in the unlikely scenario of the wings being fixed in the fully swept back position the aircraft can still be landed safely.

The Tornado features two main fuselage fuel tank groups, each supplying one engine, with the option for an additional large volume external fuel tank to be carried. Before a flight the fuel system is refuelled from a single standard NATO connector, or in flight via a refuelling probe mounted alongside the cockpit. These were detachable in the early Tornados, although the GR4 has a retractable fuel probe on the Starboard side (the pilot's right) while the F2/F3 ADV is equipped with a built-

An electrician at work on the aircraft's wiring at the Messerschmitt-Bolkow-Blohm production line in Germany. (MBB)

in retractable probe on the port side. The refuelling and feed systems are normally automatic, but the pilot can control cross feed and isolating valves in the event of combat damage or a systems malfunction.

Within the cockpit the crew oxygen system is based on a liquid oxygen converter which supplies a mixture of air and oxygen via a regulator fitted on the ejector seat, and each seat is fitted with an emergency oxygen bottle. In the event of a bail-out the canopy is jettisoned and powerful rockets fire the Martin Baker ejector seats, even at zero altitude or speed, lofting the

navigator and pilot in quick succession clear of the aircraft.

One of the less glamorous aspects of the Tornado is the approach to repair and maintenance. The aircraft has over 400 access panels covering more than 40 per cent of its surface, and a policy of Line Replaceable Units (LRUs) means that electronic components can be swapped over in a matter of minutes. Maintenance is further supported by inboard monitoring and Built In Test Equipment (BITE), all factors that contribute substantially to minimize aircraft down times and operational costs.

POWERPLANT

To provide an engine for the MRCA project a competition was held, and in September 1969 the RB199-34 turbofan was selected. For the production of the new engines another international consortium was created, Turbo-Union, which consisted of Rolls-Royce of the UK with a 40 per cent share, Motoren und Turbinen Union (MTU) of Germany with another 40 per cent, and Fiat (now Avio) of Italy with 20 per cent.

Initial development of the RB199 turbofan had begun with the Rolls-Royce RB211 concept for a civil jet engine using three separate rotating spools for low, intermediate and high-pressure – a design that provided

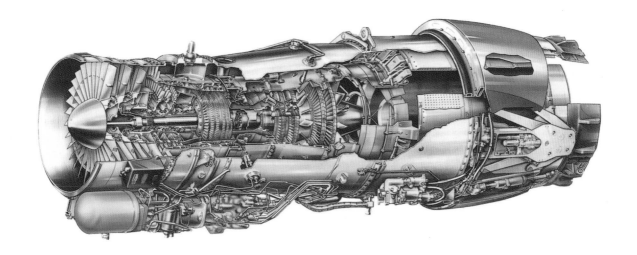

an impressive power ratio while keeping the engine small and contributing significantly to the Tornado's compact design. As a multi-role aircraft the Tornado would require an engine with economic fuel consumption at maximum dry setting for low-level transonic flight, and high reheat thrust for short take-off characteristics as well as Mach 2+ flight speed and high maneuverability.

The three-spool design of the RB199 met these requirements as each section of the engine could run at optimum speed without the need for variable blading. The result was a high compression ratio of over twenty-

'The Turbounion RB199 is a collaborative engine between Rolls-Royce, MTU and Avio designed to power all variants of the Tornado multi-role combat aircraft. The RB199 was the first-ever three shaft turbofan and incorporates an afterburner and integral thrust reverser.'

Rolls-Royce

three, plus turbine entry temperatures of over 1,600°C and reheat temperatures in excess of 1,900°C. Consequently, the RB199 is a small light-weight engine with a thrust to weight ratio greater than eight, a dry thrust of more than 8,000lb (3,630kg) and a powerful reheat that churns out 15,000lb (6,800kg) of thrust. Another innovation was the use of an all-welded disk assembly, which reduced both weight and a potential source of vibration. The blades can be replaced by cutting and welding.

The first successful bench run of the new engine was made in September 1971, and subsequent testing enabled engineers to resolve initial problems with surging and strengthening of the turbine disk. Flight testing was undertaken with the RB199 slung beneath the last of the RAF's Vulcan B1s in service, and before the P.01 prototype MRCA made its maiden flight the engines had already run for over 2,000 hours on the ground and 320 hours in the air. Development continued and the RB199 was fitted to operational aircraft in three main variants: the Mk103 for the IDS, the Mk104 for the ADV and, since 1989, the MK105, which produces an astounding 16,800lb (7,620kg) of thrust with reheat for the ECR. Over 2,500 RB199 engines have been produced and nearly six million flying hours accumulated, confirming the

Close-up of RB199 fan blades. (MTU)

13

*Full afterburner testing.
(MTU)*

Did you know?
The fuselage of the
Tornado has over 400
access panels for easy
maintenance. If only
cars were built like
this.

RB199's exceptional record of reliability and ruggedness.

True to the Tornado's guiding principle of Line Replaceable Units (LPUs), replacing an entire engine installation is a simple operation even in field conditions with the RB199 weighing in at only 2,000lb (907kg) which, by comparison, is only half that of the engine for an F-111. To accomplish this a lower engine fairing shell is opened and, with the quick-release engine mounts undone, the engine can be lowered via a pair of hand-cranked mini-hoists onto a trolley. A replacement can then be hoisted into position.

➤
Luftwaffe engineers at work on an RB199 in the workshop. (MTU)

Raw energy from the twin
RB199s of a departing
RAF GR4. (James
Vaitkevicius)

On 14 August 1974 the first prototype of the Tornado Interdictor/Strike (IDS) took off from Manching air base in Germany. Painted in a bright red and white high-visibility colour scheme, P.01 was flown by the Project Pilot MRCA Paul Millet, with Nils Meister in the back seat. Nine flying prototypes were built to test various aspects of the aircraft's systems and performance. The first British prototype, P.02, flew from Warton in Lancashire in October that same year.

Royal Air Force GR4 full frontal. (Martin Hronsky)

➤

The first British prototype P.02, XX946, at BAC Warton in Lancashire. (Panavia)

➤➤

Tornados at the Tri-national Tornado Training Establishment (TTTE) at Cottesmore, UK. (Panavia)

The contract for the Batch 1 production aircraft was signed in July 1976, and the first were delivered to the RAF and Luftwaffe in June 1979, while the Aeronautica Militare Italiana (AMI) received its first aircraft in September 1981. From the outset the IDS was designated by the RAF as the GR1, until a Mid-Life Upgrade (MLU) in the 1990s when it subsequently became the GR4. The Ministry of Defence (MoD) had originally proposed this comprehensive upgrade in the 1980s, and the program was finally launched in 1993 with the first flight of an upgraded GR4 on 4 April 1997, and the first aircraft delivered to the RAF later that year. Subsequently 142

British GR1 Tornado of No.XV Squadron, 1987. (USAF)

Luftwaffe IDS, 43+38. (Panavia)

21

Royal Air Force Tornado during the 1988 NATO aircraft display at RAF Mildenhall. (USAF)

'There is plenty of rancor between fighter and bomber crews, which is partly in joke and partly serious. Bombers are 'mud-movers' in the view of fighter crews, scuffling in the dirt, while we command the skies... Fighter pilots are the glamour boys, up at 20,000ft, monarchs of all they survey.'

Flight Lieutenant John Nichol - 'Team Tornado'

aircraft were upgraded between 1997 and 2002, after which the GR1 designation was abandoned.

The MLU included Forward-Looking InfraRed (FLIR), wide angle Heads-Up Display (HUD), improved cockpit displays, night-vision capabilities, improved avionics and weapons systems, computer upgrades and a GPS receiver. These improvements facilitated the integration of the latest

◄
Second IDS production aircraft, ZA321 in RAF colours, during a test flight from Warton. (BAC)

Did you know?
The last Vulcan B.1 in service became a flying testbed for the RB199 jet engines that power the Tornado.

weapons systems, including Storm Shadow and Brimstone, as well as reconnaissance equipment such as the Reconnaissance Airborne Pod for Tornado (RAPTOR).

The impetus to go ahead with the upgrade had largely resulted from the RAF's experience during the 1991 Gulf War. Nearly sixty GR1s had been deployed to air bases in Bahrain and Saudi Arabia but, because they lacked the equipment for laser guided bombing, they had been forced to rely on the old Blackburn Buccaneers to act as designators. With the RAF's continued operations in the region the upgraded GR4s made their operational debut in Operation Southern Watch, flying from Kuwait to patrol parts of southern Iraq, and they saw further action during

◄◄
In-flight refuelling of a German IDS over England in 1997. (USAF)

▲
Left: *Pre-flight refuelling with standard NATO connector. (USAF)*

Right: *Luftwaffe Tornado, 43+98.*
(James Vaitkevicius)

the Iraq invasion in 2003 (see *In Combat* section).

The RAF commissioned a reconnaissance version of the IDS, the GR1A, which first flew in 1985, and was later upgraded to the GR4A. In addition there was the GR1B variant which was a specialised maritime strike aircraft operating out of RAF Lossiemouth. These aircraft replaced the aging Buccaneers in this role and carried the Sea-Eagle anti-shipping missile, but they lacked the ability to track shipping and relied instead on the Sea-Eagle's seeker for target acquisition. By the 1990s the threat from surface vessels was less significant and so there was never a corresponding version of the GR4.

For Germany the main variant of the IDS was the Electronic Combat Reconnaissance (ECR) derivative, with the Luftwaffe taking delivery of 247 IDS, including thirty-five ECRs. In addition the Marineflieger of the West German Navy also received 112 IDS variants for its two Tornado units, although these have since been disbanded and their role assumed by the Luftwaffe. The German aircraft have had two upgrades of their own, known as ASSTA 1 and 2. German Tornados took part in the NATO operations during the Kosovo conflict, and more recently in Northern Afghanistan.

The first Italian prototype flew at Turin in December 1975 and in total the Italian Air Force received 100 IDS of which fifteen were later converted to ECR versions. Italian Tornados participated in the Gulf War in 1991 and in Kosovo in 1999, with the IDS being deployed in bombing missions and the ECR for the suppression of anti-aircraft radar. The AMI also leased

Four Tornados of the Royal Saudi Air Force (RSAF) with distinctive desert camouflage. (Panavia)

'Red Devils' IDS of the 154th Squadron of the Aeronautica Militare Italiana (AMI), at Ghedi. (Panavia)

Saudi Arabia, as a result of the Al Yamamah I contract in 1985 which included the sale of forty-eight IDS and twenty-four ADVs. The first of the Royal Saudi Air Force (RSAF) IDSs were delivered in March 1986 and the first ADVs delivered in 1989. Later on the Al Yamamah II contract provided for a further forty-eight IDSs, and the Saudis have also signed a contract to upgrade their Tornados and reportedly intend keeping the aircraft operational until 2020.

A major variant of the Tornado, the ADV, was instigated by the UK's Ministry of Defence as a long range fighter/interceptor to replace its Lightnings and Phantoms. Known as the F2 at first, and then, after further modifications, the F3, the ADV is far enough removed from the IDS to be considered as a new aircraft, and accordingly it is covered later in this story.

twenty-four Advanced Defence Variant (ADV) Tornados from the RAF.

The only country from outside of the tri-national partners to purchase Tornados was

Throwing thirty tons of flying machine about the sky has been described by one Tornado crew member as 'the ultimate white-knuckle ride'. Of course in reality it takes two to fly a Tornado, the pilot and behind him the navigator, or Weapons System Officer (WSO) as they are more correctly termed.

In preparation for a sortie the WSO transfers coordinates from the flying charts via a computerised Rapid Data Entry system on to an ordinary audio cassette, recording all waypoints or targets. State-of-the art technology in the 1970s, this tape feeds information into the Tornado's main navigation computer. Then he goes out to the waiting aircraft where the ground crew will have already loaded fuel and external stores. Before climbing the ladder up to the cockpit the pilot makes a visual inspection of the aircraft and signs the form that releases it into his care. Meanwhile the WSO programs the load information – which weapon is on which pylon – into the weapons control system located beneath an access panel on the fuselage.

Once the pre-flight checklist, with its 200+ litany of challenges and responses, has been completed the twin engines are

Close-up of the retractable refuelling probe on an RAF GR4. (Stephen Messe)

Tornados from the three nations line up for the opening day of the TTTE at a misty Cottesmore in January 1981. (BAC)

fired up one after the other, their whines soon developing into full-throated roars of power. 'Closing canopy', warns the pilot, and the canopy alarm sounds as it is lowered into place. The pilot releases the brakes to taxi to the end of the runway. Then it's on with full throttle to generate 30,000lb (13,600kg) of thrust which hurtles the aircraft down the runway at 180mph (290km/h) and into the sky.

The pilot's role is to fly the aircraft, monitor its systems, engage ground targets and handle air-to-air combat. Green symbols on the Heads-Up Display (HUD) show horizon indicators, altitude, heading and targeting information. Meanwhile, in the rear seat the WSO is faced by a central circular radar screen which displays either a moving map combined with radar, or radar only. Two further rectangular screens, or

'Tabs' as they are known, are situated on either side and display the mission route plan and current navigation information throughout the flight. Four sensors provide the main computer with data on the aircraft's heading, attitude, speed – including Mach number – altitude and velocity, enabling the crew to reach their target flying in any weather conditions. On auto pilot the automated computer system can maintain low-level flight using a Terrain-Following Radar (TFR) to avoid obstacles and minimise the aircraft's radar presence.

All air-to-surface weapons are controlled by the WSO. Nearing the target the appropriate weapon is released at the press of a button, but no conventional bomb-sight is required as the computerised system releases the loads with devastating accuracy.

With one type of aircraft operated by three separate air forces, plus a navy, it was decided early on that training on the Tornado was best undertaken with a joint training program and accordingly the Tri-national Tornado Training Establishment (TTTE) was established at RAF Cottesmore, in Leicestershire, to provide squadron level training for all aircrew. It opened in January 1981, and the unit was built up to a strength of fifty aircraft from the UK, Germany and Italy. The standard main course lasted nine weeks, with a further nine-week flying phase. It was a deliberate policy to pool the aircraft and to mix the instructors and students so that a British pilot might find himself flying with a German instructor in an AMI aircraft. By the late 1980s the size of the unit was reduced, in keeping with the demand for training, and the TTTE

Did you know?
Ten prototypes were built to test the Tornado's design. Nine flew and the tenth was a static test airframe.

*Formation flight of
RAF and Luftwaffe IDS
Tornados from the TTTE
in 1981.*

An Italian crew prepares their Tornado for flight. (Andreas Agostini)

▲
Interior of IDS cockpit showing the pilot's controls and instruments. (Michal Kaczmarek)

➤
An RAF Tornado sweeps past during a low-level training flight. (Rob Howarth)

was finally disbanded in 1999, with the Luftwaffe transferring its training to the USA, while the UK crews continued theirs at RAF Lossiemouth.

Training and keeping Tornado crew at combat standard requires the replicating of combat conditions, and that inevitably involves a lot of low-level flying. As Gulf War pilot Flight Lieutenant John Peters once commented, 'The only way to acquire the skills that will make you a successful bomber or air defence pilot in wartime is to push progressively to the limits while training in peace time.' The UK Military Low Flying System (UKLFS) covers the whole of the UK, although highly populated areas are avoided, and instead the aircraft fly in more remote locations such as the 'Mach Loop' weaving through the Welsh Mountains, the Scottish Borders or the deep valleys of the Lake District. The MoD states that 'Military

➤

Thumbs up from a female navigator from the RAF's No.12 Squadron during exercise Strong Resolve in Portugal, 1998. (USAF)

fixed-wing aircraft are judged to be low flying when they are less than 2,000ft (610m) above the ground.' In reality that might mean as little as 100ft (30.5m) on occasions, their appearance heralded only by the sudden roar of engines as they screech past at speeds in excess of 400mph (645km/h). Whether you are exhilarated or annoyed depends upon your point of view, but low flying remains an essential and highly demanding skill for the Tornado crews. And it's one hell of a ride!

'TTTE was officially opened on 29 January 1981 and consisted of three squadrons of Tornado aircraft flown by staff and students from all three participating countries. This arrangement proved to be a huge success and at its height TTTE trained 300 crews a year.'

RAF Cottesmore

The Tornado is designed to carry a heavy load of external armaments, or 'stores' as they are known, and, in line with its multi-role remit, these cover a diverse range of weaponry to cover every possible mission – including nuclear strikes.

From the outset the designers ensured that the Tornado would be compatible with all NATO weapons, and for the British government this initially included the WE.177B free-fall nuclear bomb with a 500 kiloton yield which was previously carried by Vulcan bombers. In theory US nuclear weapons were also available to the Germans under a dual-key arrangement with the USA/NATO. Thankfully the nukes were never needed and the WE.177B was withdrawn in 1998 with the UK's nuclear capability entrusted to the Trident missile submarine program instead.

More conventional armament is mounted on three weapon racks, or hard points, beneath the fuselage and on two main outboard pylons, and the make-up of these has inevitably evolved over many years

Test firing of the 27mm Mauser cannon which can churn out an impressive 1,700 rounds per minute. (Panavia)

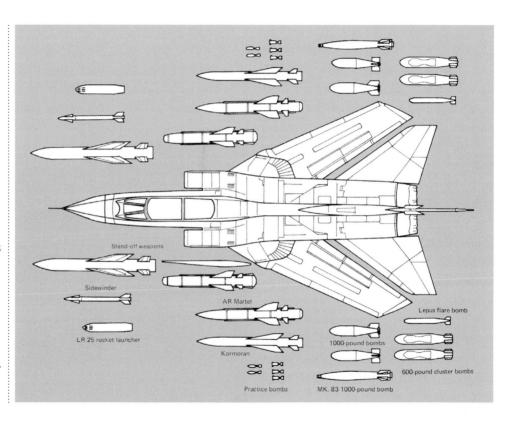

Diagram from the Panavia brochure for the IDS which illustrates the range and quantity of standard stores that can be carried. (Panavia)

Did you know?

Two prototypes were lost in service. Britain's P.08 crashed in 1979 during simulated bombing maneuvres, and Germany's P.04 crashed during an air show practice in 1980.

Stand-off weapons

Sidewinder

AR Martel

LR 25 rocket launcher

Kormoran

Practice bombs

MK. 83 1000-pound bomb

1000-pound bombs

600-pound cluster bombs

Lepus flare bomb

This pre-production aircraft PS-16 in German Navy colours is carrying the MW-1 multi-purpose weapons dispenser. (MBB)

in service. For example, the IDS could typically carry a range of bombs with up to eight 1,000lb high-explosives in tandem pairs, plus an external fuel tank beneath the aircraft's belly – or, in the case of the Paveway laser-guided bomb, the maximum was one per weapon rack.

As demonstrated in the Gulf conflict, an important mission in modern warfare is counter-airfield strike aimed at disabling

enemy airfields. RAF Tornados can be equipped with Hunting JP233 bomb dispenser pods mounted under the fuselage, each of which can deliver thirty x SG3657 parachute-retarded concrete-cratering bombs plus 215 x HB875 area-denial mines designed to deter any attempts to make repairs, all in a single low-level run.

The MMBs MW-1 munitions dispenser did a similar job for the Luftwaffe. This

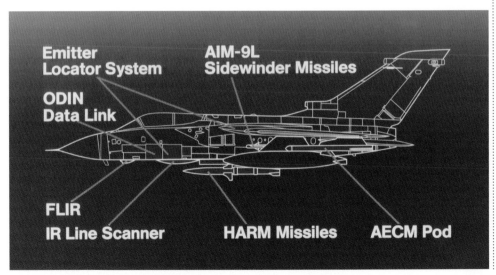

◄
Diagram showing FLIR and IR scanner, ELS, ODIN plus AIM-9L Sidewinder and HARM missiles and the AECM pod. (Panavia)

bulky 17.3ft (5.3m) long unit is loaded with 112 munitions which are ejected sideways simultaneously to cover a wide dispersal area. For anti-armour missions it is loaded with a mixture of KB44 armour-piercing, MIFF anti-tank and MUSA fragmentation munitions, whereas for an attack on an airfield it contains StaBo runway-cratering bombs, MUSPA area-denial mines, MIFF and MUSA bomblets. As with the JP233, this dispenser can be jettisoned after an attack for a rapid getaway.

A recent RAF inventory of the GR4's weaponry indicates that it can operate with up to three Paveway II, two Paveway III or Enhanced Paveway Laser and Global Positioning System Guided Bombs (LGBs), and coupled with a Thermal Imaging Airborne Laser Designation (TIALD) pod it is able to self-designate targets for LGB delivery. The GR4 also has a ground-mapping radar to identify targets for the delivery of conventional 1,000lb bombs and BL755 cluster bombs. All GR4 aircraft are capable of launching Air Launched Anti-Radiation Missiles (ALARMs), which home in on the emitted radiation of enemy radar systems, for the suppression of enemy air defences.

Currently GR4s can also carry Storm Shadow missiles, and will soon be equipped with the new Brimstone missile. Storm Shadow will allow the Tornado to make precision strikes in poor weather with a greatly increased stand-off range from the target area, whereas Brimstone will provide the Tornado with an effective anti-armour weapon.

The ADV or F3 boasts its own array of missiles, including the British Aerospace

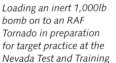

◄
Loading an inert 1,000lb bomb on to an RAF Tornado in preparation for target practice at the Nevada Test and Training Range in the USA. (USAF)

GR4 of No.31 Squadron of RAF Marham, fully loaded with external stores and fuel tanks. (BAe)

(BAe) Skyflash semi-active radar-homing missile, developed from the AIM-7E Sparrow. In the months before the 2003 Gulf War, a small number of Tornado F3s underwent a modification program to allow them to operate in the Suppression of Enemy Defences (SEAD) role. This permitted the loading of a pair of ALARM missiles in place of the Skyflash or Advanced Medium Range Air-to-Air Missiles (AMRAAMs) commonly known as 'Slammers' in USAF service, but in the event the modified aircraft were not deployed.

When it comes to self-protection the Tornado can certainly stick up for itself. The IDS is armed with a pair of integral high-velocity 27mm Mauser cannons, one either side of the forward fuselage and each capable of firing 1,700 rounds per minute, although it should be noted that the ECR

> 'Clearly, the Tornado is living up to the expectations of those who drafted the requirements for a Multi-Role Combat Aircraft back in the 1960s.'
>
> *Warplane* magazine

variant has no cannon at all while the ADV F3 has just the one as the space normally occupied by the Port side cannon is taken up by electronics displaced by the integral refuelling probe. The GR4 is frequently armed with two AIM-9L Sidewinder infra-red guided short-range air-to-air missiles, a BOZ-107 pod on the right wing to dispense chaff and flares and a Sky Shadow-2 electronic counter-measures pod on the left wing.

Kormoron, Sea Eagle and AGM-88 HARM missiles are covered in the *Maritime Strike* section.

ECR – ELECTRONIC COMBAT & RECONNAISSANCE

The Electronic Combat & Reconnaissance (ECR) derivative – better known in Germany as the *Elektronische Kampffuhrung und Auklarung* (EKA) – was developed to fulfill the Luftwaffe's electronic warfare requirements and, in particular, the Suppression of Enemy Air Defences (SEAD). The project was approved by the German government in May 1986 with an initial order for thirty-seven aircraft, the first being delivered in 1990. Germany's ECR aircraft consisted of the first two prototypes and the last thirty-five IDS airframes.

To the naked eye the ECR appears little changed from the IDS, apart from the addition of the Forward Looking Infra-Red (FLIR) sensor fairing under the nose and the absence of the Mauser cannon, but under the bonnet it is crammed with some very advanced electronics; in particular the Emitter Locator System (ELS), Infra-Red Imaging Systems (IISs), an ODIN operational data link, plus increased computing power. Although the space usually occupied by the cannon is taken up by electronics, the ECR can still pack a punch with up to four AGM-88 HARM anti-radar missiles.

The ELS system, developed by Texas Instruments, is capable of identifying a number of hostile or 'threat' radar emitters, and in reconnaissance missions aids in the identification of mobile targets and targets of opportunity. The ELS is augmented by a panoramic horizon-to-horizon internal IIS to provides high-resolution thermal coverage of the terrain being flown over, and is connected via a databus to the main computer feeding the Weapons System Officer (WSO) with navigational and control data overlaid with tactical information.

Did you know?

In the 1970s it was considered state of the art to record a Tornado's flight plan on a standard cassette tape at the Cassette Preparation Ground Station (CPGS).

A clutch of Luftwaffe ECRs in flight. (MTU)

This data can be transferred in digital format to other aircraft and to ground forces via the ODIN link. The IIS is augmented by a forward-facing Carl-Zeiss FLIR under the nose for infra-red imaging.

Two ECR units were formed, Jagd 38 at the Jever base, and Jagd 32 at Lechfeld which includes 322 Staffel whose distinctive insignia of the dragon has earned them the name 'The Flying Monsters'. Luftwaffe

Note the absence of the Mauser cannon on this Luftwaffe ECR 46+54. (USAF)

ECRs became the first German aircraft to participate in a war zone since the Second World War when eight, based at Piacenza, Italy, flew in support of NATO's Deny Flight and Deliberate Force operations over Bosnia in 1995 and 1996. Operating under the Einssatzgechswader 1 umbrella these aircraft never fired their missiles in anger but they did support air strikes by providing anti-radar cover.

The Aeronautica Militare Italiana also wanted SEAD capability following their experience in the Gulf, and twenty IDSs were modified in 1992 to carry HARM. These are known as IT-ECRs, although as modifications they retained their original RB199 Mk.103 engine. To some extent this was only an interim measure, and a further sixteen IDS conversions were ordered with full SEAD equipment incorporating Advanced Radar Warning Equipment (ARWE) produced by the Italian company Elettronica. The Italian IT-ECRs were deployed alongside their German counterparts in Bosnia.

German ECR with probe extended ready to take on fuel. (USAF)

The Tornado GR1B was a specialised anti-shipping variant of the Tornado IDS or GR1 operated by the RAF from the mid-1990s. Up to that point the maritime strike and defence role for the UK was being performed by the aging fleet of Buccaneers armed with BAe/Matra Martel missiles and later the Sea Eagle sea-skimming anti-ship missile.

As the GR1B's airframes are standard IDS variants, externally it is impossible to tell them apart from the GR1, except for their primary weapon of up to four Sea Eagles, some mounted on extra fuselage pylons. Internally an ex-Buccaneer missile control panel has been added in the rear cockpit position and new computer software was developed to handle the missiles. The first batch of aircraft could only point and shoot the Sea Eagle at a target, and, consequently, they were limited

➤

Pre-production aircraft PS-16, in German Navy two-tone grey camouflage colours with 'Marine' on the tail. (BAe)

Did you know?
No.9 Squadron's emblem is a bat, and reflects their motto '*Per noctem volamus*' or 'We fly by night'.

to line-of-sight attacks. However, this short-coming was soon rectified and later versions could download target information on to the missile's computer and launch an attack over the radar horizon in 'fire-and-forget' mode.

Two squadrons, based at RAF Lossiemouth in Scotland, operated the GR1B Tornado; No.12 Squadron and No.617, the 'Dam Busters'. However, both are now equipped with the GR4. By the time of the Mid-Life Upgrade (MLU), in the late 1990s, it was judged that a specialised anti-shipping variant was no longer needed. There was no GR4B version of the GR4, as it was already capable of carrying the Sea Eagle, and accordingly the designation GR1B was abandoned.

Germany's naval air arm, the Marineflieger, bought 112 Tornados IDS (twelve of which were dual control trainers) to fulfill its role in patrolling the strategically important Baltic Sea. Two Marinefliegerschwader units were formed, MFG 1 at Jagel and MFG 2 at Eggebek, and became operational in 1984 and 1986 respectively. Painted with a two-tone Basalt grey and pale grey camouflage scheme, these aircraft were equipped with twin AS-34 Kormoron air-to-surface anti-shipping missiles, and they could also carry the AGM-88 HARM missile. After firing the Kormoron, which had been specially developed by Messerscmitt Balkow-Blohm (MBB), the missile would descend to its target at just 10ft (3.0m) above the water to deliver a killer blow, detonating a 352lb (160kg) warhead after penetrating up to three inches (8cm) of armour plate.

Many of the Marineflieger aircraft were equipped with the 'Buddy-Buddy' in-flight refuelling system to extend their range and

A Marineflieger Tornado of MFG 1 refuels its Italian counterpart in-flight via the 'Buddy-Buddy' system.

duration, consisting of a supplementary fuel pod beneath the fuselage which could refuel fellow aircraft.

Undoubtedly the German Marine Tornados represented a force to be reckoned with, but, as with the RAF, the threat of attack from surface vessels was perceived to have significantly diminished. MFG 1 was therefore disbanded in 1993 and, although this increased the number of MFG 2 aircraft to sixty, these too were disbanded in 2005. Maritime duties were transferred to the Luftwaffe with an upgraded unit of Tornados equipped with Kormoran II and AGM-88 HARM missiles.

The Italian Air Force also operate Kormoron equipped IDS in the maritime strike and interdiction role, patrolling and protecting Italy's extensive Mediterranean coastline.

Marineflieger Tornado photographed on the flight line at Air Fête '84 held at RAF Mildenhall. (USAF)

Attempts by Panavia's original partner countries to agree upon a common dedicated reconnaissance version of the Tornado IDS were thwarted by their differing requirements and, consequently, the UK proceeded with the GR1A, which was designated as the GR4A following the MLU. The RAF initially ordered thirty GR1A's, either as new airframes or rebuilds, and the first of these entered service in 1989. Twenty-five were later upgraded to GR4A standard, and the RSAF also operate GR4A reconnaissance aircraft.

The GR1A/GR4A is equipped with two internally mounted systems; the Tornado Infra-Red Reconnaissance System (TIRRS), which consists of two side looking Infra-Red Line Scan (IRLS) sensors, visible on the lower side of the fuselage as brick-coloured glass windows beneath the WSO's position, and the primary panoramic Vinten Type 4000 IRLS, mounted in a blister on the underside of the fuselage. This equipment takes up the space normally occupied by the twin cannon, but in all other respects these aircraft retain the offensive capabilities of the GR1/GR4.

They can also carry externally mounted pods such as the Digital Joint Reconnaissance Pod (DJRP), which provides detailed

➤

A GR4A reconnaissance aircraft of XIII Squadron featuring commemorative artwork for their ninetieth anniversary in 2005. (James Vaitkevicius)

'Long range reconnaissance at all altitudes is essential to the planning and assessment of ground and air operations. With its long range, long loiter, high speed and self defence capability the Tornado makes an ideal reconnaissance vehicle to carry the sophisticated equipment involved...'

Panavia Tornado brochure

▲
Close up of the British Aerospace TIALD reconnaissance pod. (BAe)

potential. The TIRRS equipment will also be phased out. Consequently the RAF's Tactical Reconnaissance Wing, based at Marham, Norfolk, comprising of squadrons No.2 and 13 (the last of the Tornado squadrons to be formed), now fly both GR4A and GR4 aircraft as the GRA4's sensors specific to the reconnaissance role are no longer essential.

RAPTOR contains a dual-band visible and infrared sensor which is capable of detecting and identifying small targets from either short or long range and from medium or high altitudes, day or night, and offers superior haze-penetration in poor weather conditions. The optical sensors gather high-resolution motion-free images of extraordinary detail, and these can be transmitted via real-time data-link to image analysts at a ground station, or via a

reconnaissance imagery – although this is being replaced with the RAPTOR system, built by BF Goodrich Aerospace, which offers even greater day and night reconnaissance

In the foreground is a GR1A reconnaissance aircraft of No.2 (AC) Squadron flying over Kuwait near the Iraqi border in 1998. (USN)

Did you know?

Although the Tornado
is capable of speeds of
Mach 2.2, the speed of
sound is not constant
and varies with factors
such as different air
density at different
heights.

video display to the WSO enabling in-flight verification of target acquisition. RAPTOR can create images of hundreds of separate targets in one sortie, either in autonomous operation against pre-planned targets, manually for targets of opportunity, or to select a different route to the target. The imagery can also be recorded on digital tape for post-flight analysis. The stand-off range of the sensors allows the aircraft to remain outside heavily-defended areas, to minimise exposure to enemy air-defence systems.

In the mid-1990s forty of the Luftwaffe's Marineflieger IDS Tornados were also equipped as reconnaissance aircraft, and these are sometimes referred to as the LRV Version. The main equipment took the form an Aeritalia/MBB pod which contained a pair of Zeiss optical wet film cameras and a Texas Instruments RS-170 IRLS. The Italian Air Force also opted for this system.

'Tornado GR4 is a world leader in the specialised field of all-weather, day and night tactical reconnaissance. The new RAPTOR (Reconaissance Airborne Pod TORnado) pod is one of the most advanced reconnaissance sensors in the world and greatly increased the effectiveness of the aircraft in the reconnaissance role. Its introduction into service gave the GR4 the ability to download real-time, long-range, oblique-photography data to ground stations or to the cockpit during a mission. The stand-off range of the sensors also allows the aircraft to remain outside heavily defended areas, thus minimising the aircraft's exposure to enemy air-defence systems.'

RAF – Reconnaissance & Maritime Patrol Aircraft

The Air Defence Variant (ADV) was developed to meet the RAF's requirement for a dedicated long range interceptor to supersede its Lightning and Phantom aircraft; one that is capable of patrolling the UK's extensive Air Defence Region, which extends all the way from Iceland out to the Atlantic and across the North Sea to the Baltic. While the ADV has much in common with the IDS they are fundamentally as different as chalk and cheese. Visually there are several obvious clues in identifying an ADV including a fuselage stretch with a longer nose-cone to accommodate the Foxhunter air-interceptor radar system, and extra space behind the cockpit to allow the carriage of four Skyflash semi-active radar homing missiles to be mounted flush against the underside (their exposed lower fins pointing downwards like a row of shark's teeth). This also has the added benefit of reducing drag and providing space for an additional 200-gallon fuel tank.

The first of three prototypes made its maiden flight at BAC Warton on 27 October 1979. The initial batches of production aircraft delivered to the RAF in 1984 were actually F2s, in effect an interim version,

'The IDS Tornado already possesses many of the characteristics of an interceptor aircraft. In the Air Defence Variant the terrain following and ground mapping radar has been replaced by the new Air Intercept radar by Marconi Avionics Systems Ltd. This radar is the most up to date and sophisticated air-to-air radar currently available.'

Panavia Aircraft

with eighteen being built while the final spec F3s were being finalised. The F2 was powered by twin RB199 Mk.103 engines, as used on the IDS, and was only able to carry a pair of underwing Sidewinders rather than the four of the definitive aircraft.

An important factor with the ADV was the improved electronics and computing capacity, which was almost twice as powerful as the IDS. By comparison with the IDS the ADV was a mid-level to high-level interceptor and, accordingly, no

◄
The old and the new; a GR1 flies alongside the Tornado F2 at the Farnborough Air Show in 1983. (USAF)

65

Prototype F2 with wings swept back, Farnborough 1983. (USAF)

Prototype ADV, ZA283, with Skyflash air-to-air missiles mounted flush against its underside. (Panavia)

longer required the same electronic fix of ground-hugging radar, requiring instead a system that detected the enemy over greater distances. Unfortunately the early ADVs experienced teething problems with the Marconi/Ferranti AI.24 Foxhunter radar and, initially, they were delivered with concrete ballasts, earning them the unflattering nickname 'Blue Circle'. The F2 aircraft were primarily used for training purposes, although some airframes were later upgraded to F3. Without the engine upgrade these were known as F2As.

The Tornado F3 made its first flight on 20 November 1985, and it entered service the following year with 152 being ordered by the RAF. The most notable improvement was the more powerful RB199 Mk.104 engines, which had an extended afterburner which in turn gave rise to an extension of the trailing edge fin. Seven squadrons were formed, although two have been subsequently disbanded in view of the perceived reduction of threat by air attack against the UK.

The F3's primary weapons are the AIM-9 Sidewinder and Skyflash missiles, along with a single Mauser 27mm cannon located on the Port side. There has been criticism of the ADV's lack of true fighter performance, but that is to misunderstand its purpose which is to intercept targets far from base, out over the North Sea or North Atlantic. As one Tornado pilot put it, 'Fighters have to shoot other aircraft down, but they aim to do so without exposing themselves to danger.' The ADV was never designed with dogfights in mind.

In 1996 the MoD initiated a Sustainability Sustainment Program (SSP) to extend the

ADV in flight showing position of four Skyflash missiles and twin wing-mounted fuel tanks. (Panavia)

Did you know?
Because of problems with the Foxhunter radar the first ADVs were delivered with concrete ballast in their noses, earning them the nickname 'Blue Circle'.

F3's useful life beyond the original 2010 out of service date. This involved the integration of ASRAAM and AMRAAM air-to-air missiles, radar upgrades, improved cockpit displays and new processor and weapon management computers. A further upgrade involved the integration of ALARM anti-radiation missiles for the suppression of enemy air defences.

The F3 made its combat debut in the 1991 Gulf War, and they continued to patrol the Iraqi no-fly zones until the invasion of 2003, with a small number modified to undertake the Suppression of Enemy Air Defences (SEAD) role, which included a carriage of ALARM in place of the Skyflash or AMRAAM missiles, although these were not deployed in the conflict. Since 1992 F3s have also been deployed to No.1453 Flight which is responsible for policing the sovereign airspace surround the Falkland Islands.

The only country other than the UK to purchase the ADV was Saudi Arabia, with twenty-four aircraft supplied as part of the Al Yamamah arms deals, the first being delivered in 1989. However, the Saudis were almost beaten to the post by their neighbours in Oman who, two years earlier, in 1987, had ordered eight aircraft, but in the event received BAe Hawk 200s instead. Germany, Jordan, Malaysia, South

➤
F3 Tornado waits in its hangar at RAF Leeming, 2008. (James Vaitkevicius)

Korea, Turkey and Canada all expressed an interest in acquiring ADVs, with Turkey ordering forty-eight aircraft at one stage. But these deals never came to fruition.

The AMI looked to the ADV as a 'bridging' fighter to fill the gap between its F-104 Starfighters and the introduction of the Eurofighter. Twenty-four F3s were leased from the RAF over a period of ten years, with the first being accepted in 1995.

However, major delays with the Eurofighter prompted the Italians to seek another alternative. Ex-USAF F-16s were selected, and the F3s were returned between 2003 and 2004. It has been suggested that the AMI experienced serviceability problems with its Tornados, but this has more to do with poor access to spare equipment and engines, at least in comparison with the RAF's capabilities.

'The air defence task of a modern air force consists of maintaining the integrity of a designated air space and denying the enemy freedom of action. The characteristics of the aircraft required to do this depend upon the area in which it is to be deployed. In the case of the United Kingdom the task is to offer long-range air defence in NATO's UK Air Defence Region, which stretches from the Atlantic Approaches to the North Sea. The normal role of the ADV is therefore patrolling large areas, using its powerful long-range radar and short- to medium-range missiles to locate, identify, track and engage multiple targets at stand-off ranges.'

Panavia Tornado brochure

◄
An F3 of the Royal Saudi Air Force taking off during Operation Desert Shield, 1992. (USAF)

TORNADOS IN COMBAT

The Tornado's combat debut came during Operation Granby, the UK's codename for operations during the Gulf War in response to Iraq's invasion of Kuwait. The first arrived in Muarraq in August 1990, then Tabuk in October and finally Dhahran, Saudi Arabia, in early 1991. Their primary role was low-level anti-airfield attacks and SEAD, before moving on to medium-level missions against other strategic targets such as bridges, fuel depots and so on.

For the initial strikes against airfields the main weapon of attack was the JP233 dispenser, with two mounted under the

➤ *Royal Air Force GR4 from No.12 Bomber Squadron flying in Iraq, September 2008. (USAF)*

Another night time mission for an RAF GR4 of No.12 Bomber Squadron over Iraq in 2008. (USAF)

Did you know?

The Tornado IDS was designed to be a potential nuclear weapon carrier to replace the RAF's Vulcan bombers.

centre fuselage of each aircraft, while, for the later missions, conventional 1,000lb (4,536kg) bombs were carried. Paveway II Air-Launched Anti-Radiation Missiles (ALARMS) were utilised in the SEAD role, but, as the Tornados were not equipped with laser target designation equipment, twelve trusty old Buccaneers fitted with Pave Strike laser pods were given a quick coat of desert sand paint and rushed to the region. Some GR1s were fitted with a Thermal Imaging Airborne Laser Designator (TIALD) system

'The Tornado was doing 450 knots fifty feet above the desert when the missile hit. A hand-held SAM-16, its infra-red warhead locked onto the furnace heat of the aircraft's engines. Some lone Iraqi's lucky day.'

Flight Lieutenant John Peters – *Tornado Down*

to overcome this short-coming. Each GR1 could carry up to three Paveway II Laser-Guided Bombs (LGBs), and the aircraft were also equipped with a pair of AIM-9 Sidewinder missiles for self-defence as well as electronic countermeasure pods.

Royal Air Force GR1As were also deployed in the Gulf to carry out low-level tactical reconnaissance missions, in particular tasked with locating Iraqi mobile SCUD missile sites (SCUD being the NATO reporting name for Soviet-built tactical ballistic missiles).

The GR1's sleeker cousin, the F3, had actually been among the first aircraft deployed to the Gulf in 1990 when twelve F3s on detachment to Cyprus were sent to Saudi Arabia to form the air defence element of Operation Granby. These were joined by more RAF and RSAF F3s, and carried out

extensive Combat Air Patrols (CAPs) over northern Saudi Arabia. However, these aircraft never saw action against hostile aircraft.

Seven Tornados were lost to ground fire during the Gulf War, six from the UK and one from Italy, including, most famously, the aircraft of RAF Flight Lieutenants John Peters and John Nichol, which was hit by a lone missile moments after a low-level run against an airfield. With the aircraft in flames the two men ejected and were subsequently held captive by the Iraqis. Beaten and paraded before television cameras in a futile propaganda bid, they later told their story in the book *Tornado Down*.

British forces remained in the Gulf region, with GR1s based in Kuwait continuing operations over the southern no-fly zone. In 1998 they also took part in Operation Desert Fox.

As so often happens, the needs of war brought about an accelerated rate of equipment development, and the MoD's Mid-Life Upgrade (MLU) was launched in particular to address the GR1's lack of laser target designator capability. The GR4 entered front line service in April 1998, operating from Ali Al Salem, Kuwait, to patrol large areas of southern Iraq during Operation Southern Watch. Its wartime

A pair of Saudi IDS Tornados flying during Operation Desert Shield, 1992. (USAF)

'Despite flying over 360 missions in Desert Storm, the F3s never managed to get a shot off; nearly half of Iraq's combat aircraft had been either destroyed on the ground or had taken refuge in Iran.'

Flight Lieutenant Ian Black – 'Desert Air Force'

debut came with Operation Telic, as the British involvement in the invasion of Iraq in 2003 was known, and GR4s from all five active RAF squadrons were deployed. This campaign saw the first use of the Storm Shadow missile, and enhanced Paveway 'smart' bombs were used to disable enemy runways. Unfortunately in March 2003 one Tornado was struck by 'friendly fire' from a US patriot missile battery, killing both crew members. The RAF's F3s also saw upgrades with improvements to the Foxhunter radar, control systems and warning receivers.

After 1991 patrols of the no-fly zones, using F3s, were carried on under Operation Resonate South, and these continued until the Iraq invasion of 2003. They were also deployed deep in Iraq, both before and after the 'shock and awe' air strikes, Operation Telic.

◄
In this dramatic shot an RAF GR4 releases flares during a combat mission over Iraq in 2004. (USAF)

◄◄
RAF Tornado on approach to land at Ali Al Salem Air Base in Kuwait, 2003. (USAF)

Royal Air Force GR4 waits for its next mission at a base somewhere in 'Southwest Asia', 2007. (USAF)

Two RAF Tornados head a formation of aircraft behind a US Air Force KC-135 Stratotanker, accompanied by an F-15 Strike Eagle and two F-16 Fighting Falcons. (USAF)

◄
GR4 from No.617 'Dam Buster' Squadron positioning for in-flight refuelling over Iraq in 2006. (USAF)

Did you know?
The Tornado was the first production combat aircraft fitted with a fly-by-wire control system.

Operations with Tornados have continued in the Gulf and in June 2008 the UK Minister of Defence, Des Browne, announced that RAF Tornados would be sent to Afghanistan to replace a detachment of Harriers in early 2009. Controversially the German government has also committed Luftwaffe Tornados to the NATO International Security Assistance Force in Afghanistan. Six ECR reconnaissance aircraft, from 51 'Immelmann', based in Jegel, northern Germany, landed at Mazar-e Sharif airport in northern Afghanistan in July 2008.

Apart from the Gulf region, Tornados from several nations have seen action during the 1990s with operations in Bosnia and Kosovo. For example, during the Bosnia conflict, German ECRs, and their Italian equivalent, provided anti-radar cover in support of NATO's Deny Flight and Deliberate Force operations of 1995 and 1996.

Did you know?

German ECRs supporting the NATO forces in Bosnia in 1995 were the first Luftwaffe aircraft to be deployed to a combat zone since the Second World War.

'The Cold War may be over, but it has left behind a world that is less predictable and, in many places, less stable. Britain and her Allies are now faced with challenges of many different kinds... The RAF needs to be able to respond swiftly and effectively to new threats and challenges ... by projecting air power and, if necessary, countering force with superior force and skill. At the same time, the RAF must retain its fighting edge by keeping pace with technology, and training to meet the changing demands of a modern battlefield... In today's world, it is a regrettable fact that there are many conflicts and fragile cease-fires waiting to explode into fighting, not just in the Gulf area but in Asia, Africa and even in Europe. The RAF must be ready to deliver flexible air power anywhere in the world.'

RAF – Role of Air Power

RAF Tornados have carried a variety of colour schemes as the approach to camouflage tends to change with the rapidity of some high street fashions. In stark contrast to the red and white candy markings of the majority of the prototypes, the GR1s were initially delivered with a wraparound camouflage of drab dark olive green and gunmetal grey, with a black radome nose-cone. This was changed to dark grey from the late 1990s onwards, and now a complete all-over medium grey Low Infra-Red (LIR) paint is the standard.

Having said that, there are plenty of examples which have deviated from the usual colour schemes. Winter camouflage has been trialed on a few aircraft participating in NATO winter exercises in Norway, and, of course, Tornados which took part in Operation Granby during the first Gulf War wore sandy desert pink and, consequently, became known as the 'Pink Panthers'. For obvious reasons all identifying marks were kept to an absolute minimum: a discreet code number on the tail. Even so,

A GR4 in all-over grey featuring the distinctive green and yellow nose flash of No.617 Squadron. (USAF)

the tradition of combat crews customising their aircraft brought to the fore some imaginative nose-art indicating the number of combat missions undertaken and, in many cases, featuring scantily clad women in risqué poses. Some of these decorations reflected the crews' pet names for their aircraft, with Emma, Nicky, Helen, Luscious Lucy and so on, but there was also room for 'Snoopy Airways' and the more macho

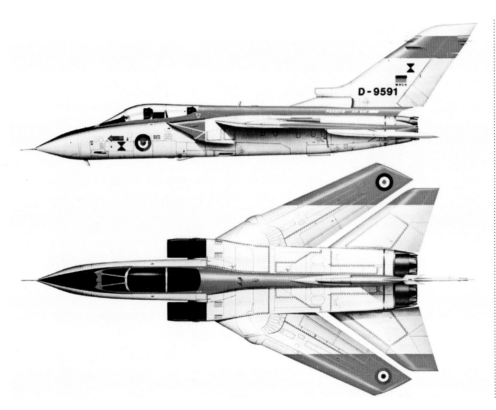

◄
Prototype P.01, D-9591, in high-visibility red and white. (Panavia)

◄◄
2003 formation flight of five specially-artworked Luftwaffe Tornados accompanied by the last remaining MiG 29 in the German Air Force. (MTU)

RESCUE

Miss Behavin'

'Miss Behavin' in desert pink with nose art. Tornados based at Dhahran had operational missions marked with palm trees instead of the usual bomb silhouettes. (Museum of the US Air Force)

operating from within the UK there is still scope to identify individual squadrons from small emblems on the tails of their craft and coordinated flash or arrowhead motifs on either side of the nose just below the canopy. These emblems are steeped in the history of the individual squadrons, such as the black bat of No.9 Squadron, the saint of No.16, the chain mail fist of No.17 and the star of No.31. Occasionally these decorations have been extended to commemorate special squadron anniversaries, with customised designs covering the entire tail fin, although in some cases these have marked the disbanding of a squadron such as the decorated F3, registration ZG780, of the 25th Squadron.

'Gulf Killer' and 'Foxy Killer'. GR4s sent to Iraq from 2003 onwards, and subsequently to Afghanistan, have been painted in all-over light grey.

Despite the standardisation of RAF camouflage paint schemes for aircraft

Other notable exceptions include various display or experimental aircraft such as the eighth production Tornado, ZA326, delivered to the Defence Research Agency (later the Defence Evaluation & Research Agency) which featured high-visibility horizontal bands of signal red, white and Oxford blue – earning it the nickname 'Raspberry Ripple'. Other specials include the jet-black ZA560, known as 'Black-Beauty', and the all-grey ZA321 display aircraft flown by the TTTE in the mid-1990s.

The Luftwaffe also identify their squadrons, or staffel, with tail emblems, plus the familiar black and white cross and the aircraft's identification numbers on either side of the fuselage. Originally Luftwaffe aircraft wore a four-colour paint scheme with black, yellow, olive and a dark basalt grey on the upper surfaces and a lighter silver grey on the undersides. However, this was later revised to a simpler all-over camouflage of dark green, medium green and light grey. Since the Luftwaffe's first return to combat, flying as part of the Deny Flight mission over Bosnia, the all-grey colour scheme has become standard. Aircraft of the Marineflieger featured a

An Italian IDS on display at the 1991 Paris Air Show. Note the red flash of the 154 Squadron 'Red Devils'. (USAF)

two-tone scheme with dark gun-metal grey on the upper half, light silver grey on the undersides and the word 'Marine' on the lower tail.

Undaunted by the need for conformity some Luftwaffe crews have found an outlet for their creativity with a number of non-standard colours, in particular for the regular NATO Tiger Meets, which feature aircraft from units with a tiger in their emblem. Some of these are elaborate works of art, with resprays featuring tiger skin patterns apparently bursting through the metal. Not to be outdone the 322 Staffel, known as the 'Flying Monsters', extended their dragon motif to cover the side of one of their ECRs.

The other two nations operating Tornados have tended to be more traditional in their approach to camouflage. The Italians used to favour a three-tone scheme of dark green, dark grey and silver broken with bright tail flashes: red for 154 Gruppo of 6 Stormo, and a yellow lightning bolt for 156 Gruppo of 36 Stormo. Originally the IDS of the Royal Saudi Air Force wore desert colours of sandy yellow, brown and dark green to blend with the sparsely vegetated landscape. Both the AMI and RSAF aircraft now conform to the all-over light grey scheme.

As anticipated, the Tornado is continuing to provide sterling service in the defence of the United Kingdom despite the disbanding of eight Tornado squadrons and the Tri-National Tornado Training Establishment (TTTE) at Cottesmore isince 1990. The remaining squadrons are based at three locations: RAF Lossiemouth in west Scotland, which is home to three squadrons, No.12, 14 and 617 (the Dam Busters) operating twelve GR4/A4s apiece, plus No.XV (Reserve) Squadron, a GR4

◄
Royal Air Force GR4 over Iraq in 2008. (USAF)

Operational Conversion Unit (OCU) with twenty-six aircraft. RAF Leuchars is also in Scotland with No.111 Squadron operating sixteen F3s, and No.56 (Reserve) Squadron, which is an F2/F3 OCU with a further sixteen F3s. The only remaining Tornado base within England is RAF Marham, in Norfolk, with four squadrons, Nos 2, 9, 13 and 31, each with twelve GR4/4As. Operating overseas the RAF also has No.1435 Flight, based at Mount Pleasant in the Falklands, with four F3s.

The MLU of the GR1s to GR4s, from the mid-1990s onwards, has ensured the aircraft's continued usefulness, and there has been some interest shown in extending their life even further with a possible upgrade of the advanced radar targeting systems. As a result there is every prospect of the GR4 remaining in active service up to 2020 and possibly even beyond, but for the F3 there is little chance of a reprieve because they are to be replaced with the Typhoon – which the British have dubbed the Eurofighter.

For the German Tornado units the writing is also on the wall. Both of the Marinefliegergeschwader are no more with the last, No.2 of Eggebek, being disbanded in 2005. And of the six land-based Jagd/Staffel only four remain active: Jagdbombergeschwader 31, at Norvenich, which has thirty-four IDSs (which are slated for a transition to Eurofighters in 2009), while Jagd 33, Buchel, is expected to replace its thirty-six IDSs with Eurofighters in 2012. However, Jagd 32 of Largerlechfeld, still have thirty-four ECRs and Auklarungegeschwader 51, Jagel/Schleswig, have forty-six IDSs which are due to receive ASSTA 2 upgrades.

RAF GR4 at full tilt. (USAF)

A line up of Luftwaffe ECRs photographed during exercises in Alaska in 2008. (USAF)

THE TORNADO AND THE LAMBORGHINI

In 2007 Lamborghini arranged a very special challenge to emphasise the exceptional accelerating power of its new aeronautically inspired and highly exclusive 1m Euro supercar, the Reventon. In true *Top Gear* style they decided to race it against an Air Militare Italia Tornado on the 1.86 mile (3km) long runway of the military airbase at Ghedi, Brescia. From a standing start the Lamborghini took the lead at first, but the Tornado caught up in the last few metres, taking-off and roaring past the Reventon which was going in excess of 200mph (320km/h)!

Italy has four Tornado units still active: No.102 and 154 Gruppo, 6 Stormo at Ghedi operating IDSs, and 156 and 12 Gruppo, 36 Stormo at Gioia del Colle, flying IDSs and F3s. 155 Gruppo, 36 Stormo based at San Damiano, also operate ECRs. In 2002 the Aeronautica Militaire Italia signed a contract with Panavia for an upgrade to eighteen of its IDSs, and a decision as to whether to upgrade or replace the remaining aircraft has yet to be made. That just leaves Saudi Arabia where the RSAF is expected to keep its ninety-six IDS active until at least 2020.

When the Tornado is finally replaced by the Typhoon/Eurofighter, or its counterparts, you can be sure that a great flying machine will have given way to an even better one. But until that day the Tornado, in its many variants, will continue to defend the territories of the UK, Germany, Italy and Saudi Arabia, serving the cause of peace in many troubled areas overseas. The last chapter might be in sight for this remarkable aircraft, but the Tornado story is still far from finished.

Did you know?
With full mission-capability, the twin-stick training aircraft are unofficially designated as GR1(T), GR4(T) or IDS(T).

RAF Tornado GR4, ZA597, with wings swept forward at an air show in the UK, 2008. (Adrian Pangstone)

➤➤
A salute for a flying legend. (USAF)

SPECIFICATIONS

Tornado IDS GR1/GR4:

Length	54.10ft	16.72m
Wingspan swept back	28.2ft	8.60m
Wingspan swept forward	45.6ft	13.9m
Height	19.5ft	5.95m
Weight empty	30,600lb	13,890kg
Max take-off weight	61,700lb	27,900kg
Powerplant	2 x Turbo-Union RB199 Mk101/Mk103	
Max speed at 36,000ft	Mach 2.2 approx, 1,452mph, 2,338km/h	
Service ceiling	50,000ft	15,240m
Rate of climb	15,100ft/min	76.7m/sec
Armament	2 x Mauser BK-27mm cannon	
	4 x fuselage pylons, 4 x underwing pylons	

Tornado ADV F3:

Length	61.3ft	18.68m
Wingspan swept back	28.2ft	8.60m
Wingspan swept forward	45.6ft	13.9m
Height	19.5ft	5.95m
Weight empty	31,900lb	14,500kg
Max take-off weight	61,700lb	28,000kg
Powerplant	2 x Turbo-Union RB199-34R Mk 104	
Max speed at altitude	Mach 2.2 approx, 1,452mph, 2,338km/h	
Service ceiling	50,000ft	15,240m
Rate of climb	15,100ft/min	76.7m/sec
Armament	1 x Mauser BK-27mm cannon	
	2 x Fuselage pylons, 4 x underwing pylons	

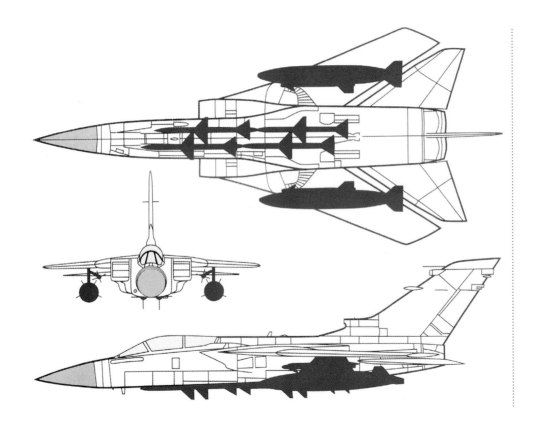

➤
RAF GR1, ZA465, on display at the Imperial War Museum, Duxford.

SURVIVORS

With the Tornado remaining an active operational aircraft it is perhaps premature to talk in terms of survivors. After all, within the UK there is RAF Lossimouth, near Moray in Scotland, which houses three operational squadrons, as well as the GR4 Operational Conversion Unit (OCU), making it the UK's main base for Tornados, in addition to RAF Marham in Norfolk, home to four squadrons operating GR1 and GR1As in attack and reconnaissance roles. And, of course, Tornados can be seen in action at many major air displays throughout the year.

In addition to serviceable aircraft there are several Tornados on static display at a number of museums both within the UK and overseas. The earliest example is P.02, XX946, which was the first of four British prototypes and is now at the RAF Museum at Cosford in the West Midlands. This aircraft, originally painted in the red and white prototype colours, first flew at Warton, Lancashire, on 30 October 1974, but was repainted in 1976 with the standard RAF all-over grey and green camouflage and given tri-national markings. After more than 600 test flights it was allocated to RAF Honington, Suffolk, in 1985, for ground crew training in weapons loading procedures. Admission is free at Cosford and the spectacular new Cold War gallery houses examples of the Lightning and the Victor aircraft.

Several GR1s are on display with both XZ631 and ZA354 at the Yorkshire Air Museum in Elvington, ZA362 at the Highland Aviation Museum in Inverness, Scotland, and ZA465 in the air space hall at

the Imperial War Museum's Duxford site. For an F3, you should visit the National Museum of Flight at East Fortune airfield in Scotland to see ZE934, operational in Saudi Arabia during the first Gulf War.

Further afield another prototype, XX948, is on display at Hermeskeil in Germany, while in the USA an ex-RAF GR1, ZA374, still in its Gulf War sandy-pink colours, resides at the USAF Museum at Wright Patterson in Ohio. For an IDS of the German Marinefliegergeschwader 1, there is 43+74 at the Prima Air & Space Museum in Tuscon, Arizona, with others in Germany at the Luftwaffenmuseum, the former RAF Gatow base in Berlin. 43+55 is at the Aeronauticum museum at Nordholz, and another at the Technikmuseum in Speyer. For the Italian-minded, an F3, MM7210, is on display at the AMI Museum at Vigna di Valle, Italy.

In addition to aircraft in museums there are a number of Tornados serving as 'gate guards' at various locations. Prototype P.03, XX947 is on duty at Shoreham Airport near Brighton, while ZA319 stands at the entrance to the MoD Defence and Distribution Centre in Bicester, Buckinghamshire, and both RAF Lossiemouth and RAF Marham have similar sentinels. You can find many more examples overseas, such as the one at the Luftwaffe base in Buechel. But do note that access to military establishments can be restricted.

XX946, the prototype P.02, at the RAF Museum, Cosford.

GLOSSARY

AAA	Anti-Aircraft Artillery
ADV	Air Defence Variant
AECM	Active Electronic Countermeasures
ALARM	Air Launched Anti-Radiation Missile
AMI	Aeronautica Militare Italiana (the Italian Air Force)
AMRAAM	Advanced Medium Range Air-to-Air Missile
ARWE	Advanced Radar Warning Equipment
ASM	Air-to-Surface Missile
ATF	Automatic Terrain-Following
BAC	British Aircraft Corporation
BAe	British Aerospace
BITE	Built-In Test Equipment
CAP	Combat Air Patrol
CPGS	Cassette Preparation Ground Station
CSAS	Command Stability Augmentation System
CVR	Cockpit Voice Recorder
DERA	Defence Evaluation Research Agency
DJRP	Digital Joint Reconnaissance Pod
DoD	Department of Defense (USA)
ECM	Electronic Counter Measures
ECR	Electronic Combat/Reconnaissance
FLIR	Forward-Looking Infra-Red
HAS	Hardened Aircraft Shelter
HDD	Head-Down Display
HUD	Head-Up Display
IDS	Interdictor/Strike
JP233	Munitions dispenser
LGB	Laser Guided Bomb

>
Tornado sunset. (BAe)

LIR	Low Infra-Red	SAM	Surface-to-Air Missile
LRU	Line Replaceable Units	SEAD	Suppression of Enemy Air Defences
MBB	Messerschmitt Bolkow-Blohm		
MLU	Mid-Life Upgrade	STOL	Short Take-Off and Landing
MoD	Ministry of Defence (UK)	TARDIS	Tornado Advanced Radar Display System
MRCA	Multi-Role Combat Aircraft		
MTU	Motoren und Turbinen Union	TFR	Terrain-Following Radar
MW-1	Meluzweckawaffe No.1 (munitions despenser)	TIALD	Thermal Imaging Airborne Laser Designator
NATO	North Atlantic Treaty Organisation	TIRRS	Tornado Infra-Red Reconnaissance System
OCU	Operational Conversion Unit	TTTE	Tri-national Tornado Training Establishment
RAF	Royal Air Force		
RAPTOR	Reconnaissance Airborne Pod for Tornado	USAF	United States Air Force
		WSO	Weapons System Operator
RSAF	Royal Saudi Air Force		

➤

Royal Air Force GR4 refuelling off the right wing of a British VC-10, Iraq 2005. (USAF)

THE TORNADO AND THE SPEED CAMERA – TRUE STORY OR URBAN MYTH?

In December 2007 several newspapers ran with a story involving two traffic police officers from North Berwick who were checking for speeding motorists on the A1. One of them used a hand-held radar device to check the speed of vehicles approaching over the crest of a hill. The radar suddenly stopped working just as a deafening roar over the treetops revealed that the radar had in fact latched on to a Tornado which was engaged in a low-flying exercise over the Border district, and he was surprised to see a recorded speed of over 300mph (480km/h). Back at headquarters the chief constable fired off a stiff complaint to the RAF Liaison office. Back came the reply:

'You may be interested to know that the tactical computer in the Tornado had detected the presence of, and subsequently locked onto, your hostile radar equipment and automatically sent a jamming signal back to it. Furthermore, an air-to-ground missile aboard the fully-armed aircraft had also automatically locked onto your equipment. Fortunately the pilot flying the Tornado recognized the situation for what it was, quickly responded to the missile systems alert status, and was able to override the automated defence system before the missile was launched and your hostile radar installation was destroyed.'